My Pain My Teacher

LEGAL NOTICES

** SAMPLE*** The information presented herein represents the view of the authors as of the date of publication. Because of the rate with which conditions change, the author reserves the right to alter and update his opinion based on the new conditions. This book is for informational purposes only. While every attempt has been made to verify the information provided in this book, neither the authors nor their affiliates/partners assume any responsibility for errors, inaccuracies or omissions. Any slights of people or organizations are unintentional. You should be aware of any laws which govern business transactions or other business practices in your country and state. Any reference to any person or business whether living or dead is purely coincidental.

Every effort has been made to accurately represent this product and its potential. Examples in these materials are not to be interpreted as a promise or guarantee of earnings. Earning potential is entirely dependent on the person using our product, ideas and techniques. We do not purport this as a "get rich scheme."

Your level of success in attaining the results claimed in our materials depends on the time you devote to the program, ideas and techniques mentioned your finances, knowledge and various skills. Since these factors differ according to individuals, we cannot guarantee your success or income level. Nor are we responsible for any of your actions.

Any and all forward looking statements here or on any of our sales material are intended to express our opinion of earnings potential. Many factors will be important in determining your actual results and no guarantees are made that you will achieve results similar to ours or anybody else's, in fact no guarantees are made that you will achieve any results from our ideas and techniques in our material.

ALL RIGHTS RESERVED. No part of this book may be reproduced or transmitted in any form whatsoever, electronic, or mechanical, including photocopying, recording, or by any informational storage or retrieval without the expressed written consent of the author.

MY PAIN
MY TEACHER

A STORY OF HOW I FOUGHT
CANCER & SURVIVED

Selina Mugodi Cheshire

Get in touch

To request Selina to speak at your event
Contact

Email; livinginthebest@gmail.com

Phone; +447584252243

Skype; Selina9600

Do you have a story to tell that could be useful to humanity and you want it published on amazon to reach millions of readers worldwide, you can get in touch with Selina on the above details

Prologue

I had my giant sisters in Christ, Florence Mutambara and Maureen, (Mai Munya) and mama maMoyo. They were always at the door of my needs. Florence my spiritual post, was always uplifting me from the depth of the pit. Maureen, being with my kids most days and nights to encourage them to be strong and even against her own judgement, reassuring them that all is well. Mama maMoyo, unbelievable love and care, you never got tired of coming to see me and feed me. You will never know how much your love and support carried me throughout the challenge. I learnt a lot too from you, giving without expecting anything back. Shylet, my cousin, my sister and my friend who went through a lot but continued to stand. Whenever she visited me with the kids, it inspired me and reminded me about who we are and what we are capable of doing.

These guys encouraged me in ways they would never understand. Shylet lost her husband at a young age and was left with 4 kids. They had gone back home after 10 years being in a foreign country and the guy lost his life after a road accident. Shylet broke her hand, kids were hurt but she survived and growing stronger every day. She symbolised a person whose belief in God never ceased, I had to be strong and live for them too. I love them and trust God for their lives. I know there are people who doubt God's power but if I think of it, even Jesus the son of God was challenged, people doubted him, some did not believe him and his own disciples, even after being around him for a long time, doubted him till his resurrection. When people visited me, I could tell that some thought I was going to die, not going to make it.

Felicity, my high school friend came for her nephew's wedding and found out that I was not well; she took time off her busy schedule to come and surprise me in hospital. Debbie, thanks love. Did not know I had a sister from another father till you graced my house, singing melodies and praying together, that was unprecedented. Tendai, oh!!! sweet sister from another mother, like we knew each other for life. Your love and trust darling is second to none. Mbuya Priscilla Nhera and family, thanks for sadza and your love which sustained me. I really could not have made it without your presence and love. You are a blessing into my life.

Julie Brierley who was my manager for a period of 10 years, saw me through my growth into Christian Science Nursing, your mentorship and encouragement, love and support kept me going. I felt a sense of belonging because of you. Yes you guided me so many times and from the darkness of my challenges, I knew and believed that I can never be left out of love. The board of Lime Tree at the time, thank you. Your visit when I was in hospital, even though it was a quick one, meant the world to me. I knew that if I was nearer Manchester you could have come more frequently. It just felt like the children of Israel receiving the benefit of Joshua's guidance and trust, everyone who visited me was led by the understanding of the Father/Mother's provision of their love, their time. MBE says 'Whatever blesses one blesses all. While the need of food and drink are legitimate, they are just like a drop of water in the ocean, every drop counts though seemingly it seems it has no significance, it matters. As the bible says,'......'Take no thought for your life, what you shall put on...' We are reminded to trust in the Lord our Father/Mother God to supply us with all our needs. These friends met all my needs. Maggie Johnson, what a joy it was to have you, left a big impression in my thoughts. You taught me to just be me and love and laugh without a worry in the world. I still remember. Last but not least, Louise you were incredible my dear. You made a difference in my understanding of Christian Scientist love. I so enjoyed our walks in the park and along the canal. Your sharing of the reading of the Bible lesson really made my life worth living.

Acknowledgement

They say having children can be a challenge and a blessing. I really want to thank you my two heroes; my son Tariro Kazembe and my daughter Samantha Ndhlela of which without you I would not be here. Your observance and love made you realise when things began to go bad. Also, to my other son Sicelo Ndhlela, your stand and support can never be faulted. Gwen Kuda, thanks baby for carrying that big suitcase full of organic food to start me off my journey. I also want to thank my son Walter and family; you were not there with me physically but I know your prayers were like bullets to the devil. My brother Joseph, in your own way, thank you for being there.

My husband Robert Cheshire, the silent warrior and my supporting angel!!!! I really appreciate you. Every day without fail you were at my bedside and yes you were pained by the human picture but you never showed it to me. Ellaine Barth, leaving your life in Switzerland to come and be with me for 5 days: love you sister.

I want also to thank Maureen Mildred, my daughter's mother-in-law who stood by my children and me all through the journey. I know sometimes things were tough because human nature always wants to take charge of the good and destroy us but united in the Lord we stand. I also want to thank my soul sister Florence Mutambara for being strong in the Lord of which your visits were full of love and encouragement. You knew that the God in me is ever present and no harm could destroy me.

To the Nheras, my aunts and uncles with their families, I will always value you. I know my mum wherever she is, is pleased. Mum MaMoyo, your unconditional love and support were second to none. You brought my late mum alive by your care and support. Tears always run down my cheeks every time I think of you. Sister Mary, thank you so much.

Finally to my Niece Gwen Mugodi and Kenneth Ejiofor who made the final script ready and published, thanks a million.

TABLE OF CONTENTS

CHAPTER 1

INTRODUCTION

There I am, sitting in front of one the most experienced oncology doctors and the atmosphere is eerie. I can only hear the tick of the clock. She looks at me right in the eye and, without a flinch, utters these words, 'Selina, if you do not have radiotherapy, you are going to die.' I believe they have done a good job to help me get where I am, but this is far from what I wanted to hear. I do not want to hear about death. Am I afraid to die? No. I am not. I am in the right frame of mind and it is so evident from the internal conversation I am having with myself. I have come a long way and this is the final straw I need to hear to validate my refusal of further medical intervention.

The Doctor urges me to reconsider, 'Think about your family,' she says to me. She adds there are a few traces of cancer cells left that need to be removed through radiotherapy. 'Well Doc, can I ask you a question?' I say. She nods her head for me to continue. 'What is the difference in terms of side effects between chemotherapy and radiotherapy?' It's clear the Doctor did not expect me to question her; she expected me to agree with her without challenge. She responds in a more aggressive manner pointing out that the Radiotherapy would target the cancer cells and the sessions would only last about 15 minutes per day for 2 weeks. At this point, she urges me once again to think about my children and the amount of time I will be able to spend with them if I complete the radiotherapy. I quietly tell her I am unwilling to continue with any further treatment and to suffer from the side effects. What has been most brutal about my Chemotherapy sessions are the side effects and I am not going to put myself through that again. I hear a soft voice repeatedly say to me 'Be not afraid, I am with you always. I am your God and your healer. The herbs of the earth shall help you find healing.' I am quiet for a few seconds but it seems like forever, when I say to her 'Thank you so much for your offer but sorry, I cannot accept it. Let me continue what I have been doing. I know it is better because I have had no after effects or side effects.' She responds 'Selina, it's your choice but let me give you my card. In case you change your mind just ring my secretary and she will book an appointment for you straight away.' I take the card and say 'Thank you, I will take it and will call you if I need to but I pray it never comes to that.' As I walk out if the consultation room I feel as if I have just been before a High Court Judge and won the case. That feeling of achievement envelopes me and gives me so much gratification.

My son is waiting outside in the car for me. 'Mum, are you ok? What happened? What did the Doc say? Are you getting radiotherapy or not?' My son is looking at me with so much compassion as well as concern. He looks similar to the actor Idris Elba, tall, dark and handsome. He looks at me and gives me a big hug, and I think to myself at that moment, 'All I need is love; unwavering love.' I fight back the tears that threaten to break loose and remind myself how blessed I am to be alive and have two brilliant children who are actively supportive. My daughter is waiting for me at home, a beautiful soul, patient but firm. She has been my anchor at my lowest points and has played a major role in my healing process. Without her, I might have let go already and gone to the Lord before my time. I think about the journey we have all travelled this far together, my children and I. I am determined to live for them. I decide in that moment to invest in myself and fight for my life. A verse from the Bible comes to me; 'I move and live and have my being in God.' That verse inspires me into a new sense of freedom I never knew I had.

Now, before we go any further, let me share with you how I came to be in this situation - ending up at the hospital facing the oncology doctor.

CHAPTER 2

The Discovery

'Though I walk through the valley of the shadow

of death, I will fear no evil' -Psalm 23:4

2014 is the year I will live to remember and be happy to forget. Prior to my diagnosis, my life was smooth, simple and joyful. I loved working with people. I was employed to nurse people with the support of prayer, seeing them as perfect children of God, created in His image and likeness. I had learnt how to pray for myself while I worked with people seeking support. I had no room for negative thought and pain was never part of my life. Having this in mind, going to the hospital or seeing a Doctor was never part of my way of life. So, when my children sat me down and asked me to see a Doctor, I was confused. The thought of seeing a Doctor while I 'felt' well, came as shock to me. The idea of seeking medical intervention never crossed my mind at all. I questioned myself and my children, why they thought I should seek medical attention. They knew as well as I did that as a Christian Science nurse[1] it was unacceptable and frowned upon to even consider the idea of engaging in medical intervention as well as spiritual healing.

My son Sibbz, stood up, held me by the hands and said 'Mum, look at me, look into my eyes, can you not see that you are sick?' He continued 'Can you walk up the stairs please? If you get to the top and are not breathless, we will not take you to the Doctor.' I felt annoyed and agitated at the request. When have I ever been breathless while walking up the stairs, or walking at all? I had not noticed any of the issues he was describing to me. Sibbz added, 'Mum, I am not arguing with you, let's walk up the stairs and you can prove me wrong. If you are breathless when we get to the top of the stairs, I am taking you to the doctor.' My daughter Sam looked at me in agreement. I felt as though I had no other choice, I had to prove them wrong by walking up the stairs without getting breathless. Unfortunately, that was a battle I lost.

---

[1] A practice where the nurse works with people who do not take medication but depend on prayer for healing in a supportive way.

I was so out of breath by the time I got to the top of the stairs that I had to sit down.

We were at the local GP (General Practice) surgery within 30 minutes' time. I had not been to a GP surgery in over 10 years and had to register as a new patient. I filled in the required forms but had to return on another date to see the doctor.

The mind is a unique machine. From the minute I was told it appeared I had breathing problems and went to the GP surgery, I started to feel pain all over. It became even harder to walk up and down the stairs. I continued to go to work and fought through the challenges I was feeling. I started to feel as though things were declining fast. I nursed myself at this point, repeating the words 'There is no life, truth, intelligence or substance matter' (Mary Baker Eddy). My faith kept me strong but the pain I was feeling in my chest was excruciating.

This period in my life was tormenting and confusing. I wanted to maintain my standards as a Christian Science Nurse. I was afraid to tell anyone at work because seeking medical attention was frowned upon. At the same time, I also did not want to disappoint my children. I could see that my children were afraid that something was terribly wrong.

I finally saw the Doctor, and was sent for a scan. At this point, my friend Robert and another friend, we'll call her Sue, had planned to go on a holiday retreat to Scotland for a couple of days. I thought some time away would help clear my mind and give me some clarity. I wanted my scan results before I went to Scotland, so on that Friday morning, I contacted my GP and was informed the results were in already, but that I needed to make another appointment to see the Doctor regarding the results. The nurse said I could come the following Wednesday, 4 days later. I found this quite distressing and could not understand why it was taking so long. At this point, I went down on my knees and prayed. I prayed and prayed. Honestly speaking, I was praying the pain away and praying for the truth of who I am in God's eyes to appear, but for some reason the pain would not subside. Instead, it increased. The whole day was so distressing because I was beginning to doubt if I would be good company to my friends. Instead of packing during the day, I just sat on my couch contemplating. It was not until 8pm in the evening that I decided to go upstairs to my room and pack for my journey up North. When I got to my room, I could not even lift my hand to pack. I just sat at the edge of the bed sobbing. The pain was so blinding I could not even think. The only thing I managed to do was call out for my children, who came rushing to my side. Seeing the state that I was in they called 999 for the Ambulance Service without even asking for my opinion; I was in agony, crying only. I remember seeing the ambulance personnel giving me something to relieve the pain. They tried all the painkillers they had but nothing worked. They had a chat with my children and agreed on taking me to the hospital. At this point I knew something was not right.

I was in grave pain; the Ambulance crew did their best to ease my pain but it would not subside. As soon as we got to the hospital we met a nurse who expressed tremendous compassion, care and love towards me. She expressed the qualities of the nurses that I work with on a daily basis. However, it took a long time for the health professionals to determine what to do with me. They had no idea what was causing the pain and discomfort. I recall my daughter telling me after the ordeal that I looked like death was knocking at my door.

Once I was admitted, they administered morphine and I finally fell asleep. I woke up in a side room on my own, wondering what in the world was happening to me. I few moments later, a nurse came into the room wearing a hospital mask. This shocked the life out of me. The little hope I had left vanished! The nurse had very little interaction with me, and just dropped off things on the table and left. At that moment I thought; how is she a nurse? Where is the compassion? After being in the general ward for 2 days, I was given a side room and a nurse entered my room wearing a mask. She never spoke to me or acknowledged me. She threw something on my table and left the room. I attempted to call her back because I needed her assistance to go to the bathroom, but she hurriedly fled. I felt so discouraged, sad and distraught that I had left the warmth of my home only to be thrust into a cold heartless hospital room. I had no buzzer to call for help if needed and the room was terribly cold. At that particular moment I thought, 'Is this what Florence Nightingale envisaged when she cared for patients and fought for patients to be treated appropriately?' Such thoughts kept flooding my mind. I was hugely disappointed in what I was witnessing and experiencing. The only way I could get help was to call my son and ask him to contact the ward reception. It took him 3 hours to get through to someone and the on-call ward manager came to see me. The manager was so understanding of my position, portrayed compassion, care and empathy which the other nurse did not show. Everything that needed rectifying was rectified. He made me feel like I was finally in the right place and could put my mind at ease and focus on getting myself out of despair.

The following day my friend Flo came to visit, she was part of my support system that always saw my heart and spoke life into me. Being a Christian Science nurse herself, she challenged the nurses to practice in the manner in which they were trained because the room was very cold when she walked in. A Christian Science Nurse works with people who do not take any medicine for healing but depend on prayer, knowing who they really are before God. Apparently, they assumed I had Tuberculosis and thought I was infectious. It took 2-3 days of tests for the health professionals to conclude that I did not have Tuberculosis. The team came, with no masks this time, to inform me that it was not Tuberculosis, but something else which they wanted to be sure with before they could do anything. They asked me if I was feeling better or needed more pain reliever. I stayed in the side room for a day or 2 waiting for further tests. I was elated now assuming that it was all over. You know that inward feeling. The ward was so busy, and it was like the nurses never had time to relax, always being needed somewhere for help but I really appreciated them, always smiling. I did not get much in the sense of medication but just morphine.

However, when I was beginning to settle in, the same team, plus some students came into my room and told me that they had just received the results from the scan my GP had requested a few weeks earlier. My daughter was with me when they came, and they asked if I would like to have her around while they break the news. I was happy for her to stay. With all the love and empathy, I was informed that I had cancer. The official diagnosis was Hodgkin Lymphoma Stage 4. Time seemed to have stood still in that moment. I was in tears and confused. I was surprised to hear my voice questioning them, 'Are you sure the results are mine? Are you not mistaken? Why now and why me?' So many thoughts ran through my head. 'My children!' I thought to myself, 'what will happen to my children?' I could not see through the dark clouds that had descended upon me. I cried so violently, I felt as though I am hearing, for the first time when I was 12 years old that my mother had died. I remembered how fearful I was and just imagining how I took on a motherly role and looked after my siblings at that tender age. At least I was back home in Zimbabwe with my dad, my grandmother and all other relatives were around us. Here in the United Kingdom, there were very few of us and people had to go to work to pay their bills. My daughter had just finished her University studies; she has a future ahead of her!!!! There was so much pain and confusion at that time, and it felt as though I was reliving that moment. All the pain and confusion were difficult to bear but I looked to my daughter and remembered the promises God made to mankind, he said "I will never leave you nor forsake you to the end of the earth." Samantha, my daughter affirmed that and promised that she will be there to support me.

The Doctor stated that we had to act now, and I needed to begin chemotherapy immediately. The cancer had produced some fluid which had covered the right lung completely and three quarters of the left lung. They proceeded to show me images of the scans of my chest. I was astonished to say the least. The Doctor was surprised at how I had managed to survive this long in such a state. I looked at my daughter for reassurance and she said 'Mum I will be here with you so don't worry. You are not alone, and you know God is with us.' Through all the pain and confusion, I felt, she gave me hope. I agreed to go ahead with the chemotherapy and after a while was moved to the Oncology Ward. Oncology was a new word to me, I had never really heard about it.

CHAPTER 3

Pain and more pain

Oncology ward, wow!!! Here you find all sorts of people, men and women sharing the same ward. Some are bald headed, some are wearing wigs and some look just normal. Some patients are in pain, could be heard audibly groaning and screaming. After being in this ward for almost 4 hours, it made me feel as though I had reached the end of my life. It appeared to be a place of pain and sorrow. I was mesmerised by what I was witnessing. It felt as though it was a place where one can come to be mended or broken. I had never spent so much time in a hospital in all my life, to the point where I made some friends and also discovered that some nurses are dedicated to their jobs and patients, always cheerful, doing what appeared to be their best and having time to encourage and give a smile. Some patients were also very encouraging and reassuring me that I will be fine and to never fear. I used a lot of inspirational thoughts I had collected previously and lots of bible verses, which I will share later.

The chemo dose was finally determined after numerous tests. The doctors did not waste time in starting administrating the chemo. I had to be prepared as well and the nurse brought a gown with an open back and helped me put it on. I was transferred onto another bed and wheeled to a room which was at the back of the ward, just away from everyone's eyes or ears. I had to lie still on my back and the nurse stood by, reassuring me all the time until the doctor walked in. He was dressed in his coat and gloves. They always reassured me that it was all going to be great. Sometimes they would find it difficult to get the veins to administer the chemotherapy. At first, I did not feel any difference from the time I started until after almost a week, when they said the chemicals were taking effect. Once I was filled up, I felt better and happy thinking I was getting healed. As days went by, my veins began to get thinner and it was becoming difficult to obtain blood. My right hand had become so swollen I could not use it and had to have it raised all the time. It was discovered that I had Lymphedema – swelling commonly caused by the removal of or damage to the lymph nodes as a part of cancer treatment. From my understanding, if a patient has Lymphedema on their hand it should not be cut in any way even by a syringe. One morning a nurse tried to take blood as always you find an odd one. I told this nurse that she should not tamper with my right hand, but she did not listen. She just plunged on and nothing came out so in the end they had to insert a cannula, I went to the theatre for it to be placed on my neck, to make it easier for them to get blood every morning. It was the beginning of stress and more pain because it became hard for me to stretch, let alone dress myself; more work for the nurses as if they did not have enough. This caused me to have what they call thrombosis on the right hand and I was only given Clexane injections which really did not help much for I continued to have challenges using it. The nurses didn't seem to care much about it since I was always in bed. I could not do much for myself anyway so why waste precious time which could be used to save another life. The other patients were amazing and always willing to share and help. Some patients, when their families came to visit, would always share the food and whatever was brought for them. We were becoming tired of the tasteless food which was cooked at the hospital, always too bland for me; I am used to chilly spicy food.

Making Friends

In the oncology ward, a variety of people came and went, some staying for a day or two, others for longer periods, like myself. I met wonderful women/ladies whose love and laughter will stay with me for a long time. We laughed and shared things about our lives before cancer. Cheryl was the youngest of the four of us who were regulars. She was only 38 years old and had had a wonderful life singing on cruise ships! Did I know one can sing and move around the world as a profession? I just felt connected to her instantly when we opened up, as we shared less painful moments. She shared some videos she had taken when her husband came to visit because he always brought her laptop and entertained us with Cheryl's beautiful voice and moves. We laughed and joked, for an hour or so we would forget why we were there. Ultimately, she did not make it. She passed on one morning without saying goodbye. Did this make me sorrowful? Yes, but I told myself that she was now in a better place where there was no fear or pain or suffering. I grieved for her for a few days then surrendered her to God the creator who is the source of all being.

Then came Shazia; gentle and full of love but also very bitter and sorrowful. She had been married and moved from her native country, Pakistan, but for the 10 years she was married, failed to have children. You could tell that she thought about it on a regular basis especially when others would be visited by their kids and no one for her. She cried so often and always asking God why she was never blessed with just one kid just to make her feel like a woman. Her husband loved her and always reassured her of his love for her. We shared, gossiped as is always the case where women come together and always pray for each other, and encouraged each other to be strong and to keep holding on to God. She was moved into a side room, which was something akin to a promotion and I enjoyed going in to visit. It seemed like she was getting better but Lord she did not last two weeks, she joined Cheryl. You can imagine how this affected me; devastating to say the least.

Shazia was gone in the morning and around midday I was asked to move into the same room. How scary and frightening! Pain, sorrow, fear, and uncertainty clouded my mind. I thought whoever was responsible for moving me into what had been friend's room just hours before was heartless and had no compassion for friends. At this juncture a passage I loved and had used so many times came to mind.

Psalms 91:2-5

2) I will say of the Lord, He is my refuge and my fortress: my God: in him will I trust.

3) Surely he shall deliver thee (me) from the snare of the fowler, and from the noisome pestilence

4) He shall cover thee (me) with His feathers, and under his wings shalt thou (I) trust: his truth shall be thy (my) shield and buckler.

5) Thou (I) shalt not be afraid for the terror by night; nor for the arrow that flieth by day;

All of a sudden fear dissipated and I was pushed into the room (at least it felt like it). It gave me a good feeling, as if I had conquered death already. I said to myself, 'God is the source of all being and if I go into there, there is only God, Shazia who is really spiritual, is gone.' The body had been moved out and nothing really could touch me. Her spirit was free now and she could not harm me. I quietly called the nurses and told them I was ready to move to the allocated room. If I say the nurse was surprised it's an understatement, she looked pale white because an hour ago I had vowed that I would never go in the 'slaughter' room. This was because everybody I knew or met had never come out alive. At first it felt as if I had signed my own death warranty.

Mary Baker Eddy's Christian Healing message came to mind. She wrote, 'If you wish to be happy, argue with yourself on the side of happiness; take the side you wish to carry and be careful not to talk on both sides, or to argue stronger for sorrow than for joy. You are the attorney for the case and will win or lose according to your plea.' Wow! Thank you, God, for the reminder. I had to take charge of my case and no fear would bring me down. I had the support and love of my family and friends, and we all know love moves mountains. I knew I had to stand firm at the door of my own thinking if I wanted to live and fight for my life. I had God on my side who created me in his own image and likeness, and nothing whatsoever could take that from me. I knew and concluded that this was my moment and so moving into the side room was the beginning of the process. I was at peace at last and the room was wonderful. I had space of my own and could spend my time in prayer and meditation, when I managed, which of course was very rare. Most of the time, I was in pain. Being in the side room was a bit different, I was free from prying eyes and people could bring whatever they wanted for me to eat. I began to send love to those who had departed and encouraged them to move on peacefully, especially my friends I had met in the ward who had just passed on. This gave me peace.

Visitors

The side room proved to be useful when a friend from Switzerland came to visit and stayed with my children for five days. What a blessing because we could talk and share our love for Christian Science which had brought us together. She would come in and read to me from the Bible and Science and Health and some periodicals. What a joy and anticipation for a good life that was. She made me feel loved and reminded me that it was not just my immediate family who cared about me. It was those who trusted and cared for me also who kept me going. Ellaine left a mark and I really do not know how to express my gratitude, only God knows, for giving her time and money to be with me, to nurse my mind and my faith and give me reason to be stronger in my understanding of God.

Felicity Ncube, a childhood friend from Zimbabwe heard that I was not well and could not go back to Botswana, where she was teaching, without surprising me. How she collaborated with my Facebook friend Deborah Mawlem, only God knows. It all happened in the side room and Florence Mutambara, soul sister and workmate at the time, k0new my love for organic food and so every time she was able to visit I knew I was having treats. My uncle George Nhera and his beautiful wife Priscilla and their family also were constant visitors in this private ward. My cousin Shylet and her crew were my favourites because I could go into the lounge and see the kids running around. My aunts, Ruth and Laina, also came to bless me. A lot of them, because of the outside picture, never thought they would see me walking again. Julie Brierley and Alister Budd, fellow Christian Nurses, came to visit but they left thinking it's just a matter of time before they hear of my passing on. I am sure most people would rather not remember that time, neither would I. But regardless of the pain, the love I got from that small room will always stay with me. I learnt the importance of having a human being around, a physical person to call on rather than just phone calls and prayers which might end up being of no value, when I was in that room. I got a lot of encouragement and felt the love of those who cared to be near me. I lost valuable friends after that but also made a lot of great new friends.

CHAPTER 4

The side effects

Sitting in my bedroom writing this now is painful. It feels as though I have been to hell and back but it has to be told. It is like writing someone else's story. What I went through in the oncology ward is hard to think about but in order for me to heal quicker, I need to tell it as it happened.

Doctors and nurses are amazing. They carry on their work as if they do not care but if you look deep into their eyes, most of them anyway, you can see the love and compassion they have for each patient. The administration of chemotherapy was scary to both the Doctor and the patient, even the nurse assisting the Doctor. The Doctor has to be covered so that none of the chemicals can go onto his shirt, let alone his skin and has to be precise. The patient on the other hand needs to be relaxed and pretend to be at peace.

As we are preparing for the drill, I would play the part, joking with them as if we are going for a swim but deep down praying like mad. I always thought of myself as being the apple of God's eye, nothing could touch me there. I would relax, while they filled me with toxins for about 20 to 30 minutes. The first day was not a bad one, it even seemed like any normal injection but after two weeks' things began to change. I started sweating at night and even during the day. My appetite was also waning but I could hear my grandmother from the time I was young saying 'Selina, eat, you are not in hospital for a holiday. If you do not eat, the chemicals will eat you up. Do not worry about the taste of the food, think about getting well and getting out I heard you granny and yes I munched my food away. The only person I could think of asking to prepare and bring different food in to me was my daughter.

A few months into the treatment, let us say about October 2014, I started having diarrhoea. I started feeling pain while tying my locks. It did not alert me that I was about to lose my hair, it just felt like something that will come to pass. I loved my hair. It looked great and I really never thought I would cut it. I love natural hair and the locks were just me. At first I ignored it but when I started seeing my locks steadily falling, I knew there was danger. It so happened that I was given a few days over the weekend to go home that my son, who loved my locks too, started screaming at me 'Mom, your hair is coming off, it's falling!!! Have you seen it mum?' So many questions were being thrown at me and to be honest, I did not have a clue that it was now visible. I was now living in my own world; a world of self-pity and pain was second nature and things like losing my hair were insignificant. I just said 'Really? Let us just ignore it for the present moment and see how far it goes.' By the end of my visit to my own home, (4 days) half my head was shaved. I ended up asking him to remove it completely and my head was now as clean as a baby's bottom.

Figure 1: Picture of me hairless

Mid November, I was allowed to have home visits almost every weekend but leaving home was becoming difficult, I had to cry every other visit, but this time I really did not want to go back into the ward. I was feeling low, temperature going up and down like a yoyo. When I got back the nurses were alarmed, they had to call the on-call doctor. Within 24 hours I started having ulcers on my mouth, inside, spreading fast down my throat and into my chest. Now I could not swallow, not even my own saliva and guess what, Friday was a day away. I knew for real that the weekend was going to be the longest because of pain if nothing was done. I shared my concerns with the nurse who came and helped me with a wash that morning. She promised to give a report to the morning doctors. Whether they were told or not will never be known because nothing was done in relation to the ulcers. Thursday night, I could not sleep. I listened to S&H (Science and Health by) Mary Baker Eddy the whole night from my smart phone which kept me sane and gave me encouragement. I tried telling the doctors when they came to do their morning round but they did not take me seriously. They thought I was just putting up a show so they left me without anything to ease the pain or even a drip to ensure a continuous flow of liquids. I had mouth ulcers on the 18 of August 2014 and diarrhoea and I was told it was one of the side effects of chemotherapy. It was so difficult to eat or drink anything. I tried the hospital food, but it tasted like medicine. The only thing I could eat was 'sadza[2]' and okra it was easy to swallow, I did not have to chew anything. My daughter learnt to do food modification which was a great help. I came to understand how important it was to try different methods of cooking as a way of helping those who are having eating challenges, not to force them to just try at whatever cost. I now understand that we all have those moments where sometimes we cannot manage to look at food and be drawn to it. I did not even know how to deal with diarrhoea so being in the side room helped. Things changed slightly as my body was getting used to the medication, but it was short lived because the side effects were kicking in which made the Doctors give me different medications.

My second episode of ulcers was from the 30th of October 2014, this really was the real deal. I had

---

[2] . Sadza is the basic food from Zimbabwe my country of birth and most of Southern Africa

ulcers on my lips and tongue, throat and in my chest. I could not swallow even my own saliva and it happened towards the weekend so did not have much attention from the Doctors. I was not given anything for it, so I had to really dig deeper into my prayer life. I called unto God from the roof tops and he heard me. I was sweating and another spat of diarrhoea started. I ended up having pads and a commode beside my bed because I could not get to the bathroom on time. I remember one night, before they thought of giving me a pad, the Nurse in charge did not have a break. I needed the loo every 30 minutes so basically it was more of a one-to-one care night. Thank God they ended up using other means. I got over it by the care and love of God. I had to take loads of water, sipping it throughout the weekend and okra juice came to the rescue. I found out that these natural foods have so much nutritional value that I do not manage to get from the normal foods we buy from local takeaways or restaurants.

Fortunately, my sister Jennifer Rugara who lives in Zimbabwe and who was in constant communication with my daughter advised her to buy okra, cut it into smaller pieces and put it in boiled water and leave it for about 20-30 minutes then give it to me to drink. It was slimy but I did not have any choice. I just told myself that it's better than nothing, my throat was killing me. That Friday from midday, whole of Saturday and Sunday, I fed on the okra concoction plus water and Ribena. This helped me get through the weekend. To my surprise, one of the nurses came to me on Monday morning and apologised because she knew they had left me without putting a proper care plan in place, they should at least have given me a drip so that I could have water. I had been left to fend for myself, but because God is amazing, I survived.

As I continued to stay in hospital, the pain and confusion continued. I began to see myself going through a very small tunnel, like going through a black hole in my own thoughts. I welcomed the idea because it felt like the only escape route left. I kept telling myself that it was the best and easiest way. Questions without answers played around in my mind. 'What will I be like after it all? I am going to be useless and a worry to my children, is that worth it? They have their own lives to live so do you think it is right to just be selfish and hang on, there must be a way for you to go?' I thought I was talking to myself and yet my daughter who was near me and who knew me now like I was part of her silently and strongly said to me, 'Mum, please do not go yet, you can do it and please we can do it together. You are a strong person and we can do it.' We were walking to the bathroom.

I did not say anything but felt guilty as a little child caught stealing sugar by her mum. I just looked sympathetically at her as if to say 'sorry, I am already gone.' 'Mum, please listen to me. I am here for you and remember I have stopped working because I want to look after you mum. Please do not do this to me.' That was my daughter calling me back. Tears begin to stream down my cheeks. 'Honey, what is the point, look at me, I am just a walking ghost.' I really felt that there was no reason for me to go on. 'Please let me go,' I said looking into my daughter's pained eyes. I was ready for this because I had been preparing myself to move into another existence for a few weeks now. 'Please Mum, do not agree to those thoughts or suggestions. You have the power to say no. Mum, please listen to me.' It was almost a plea from the heart of hearts. With a long loud sigh, I heard myself saying, 'Ok honey, you have won. Yes, we can do it.' She hugged me. Tears of joy rushed down her cheeks. She did not let me go until I softly reminded her that I had come to use the toilet.

The Confusion

With Samantha gone, left alone in my room, the confusion continued. Voices bombarded me left, right and center, 'Look at you, who do you think you are? Nothing but a weak useless person. Look at you, a walking ghost. And you say you are not going? How many medications are you on? Hahaha, you think you can do it? How many people have passed on from this same room since you have been in this ward, maybe the same bed and mattress? You will never make it. If you do, you will be useless, a burden to your kids. Remember you are in a foreign country, no other people to help your children. You want to steal their lives from them? Just let go.'

It seemed like 1 had hundreds of unanswered questions. It was like I was asleep, or rather in a trance, daydreaming. I forced myself up into a sitting position and everything started to float away. I began to pray, pray like I never did before. Praying with passion and understanding. I remembered God's promises for my life. Stories of people in the Bible Who God had used for his work. People like Jonah in the whale's belly, did not God spat him after three days? I even remembered Daniel and the Hebrew boys. Thrown into a fiery furnace but came out with no smell of fire, their clothes untouched by fire and still praising God. Were they any different from me? They were also in a foreign land just like me. God was right there with me as he was with them. The story of the woman with an issue of blood who had used all her savings to seek treatment, was not she healed by just the touch from Jesus the Christ? I felt the love of God encompassing me. A hymn from the Christian Science hymn book came to mind; Hymn 166/67 by Henry Frances Lyte:

Know, O Child, thy full salvation;
Rise o'er sin and fear and care
Joy to find, in every station,
Something still to do, or bear.

Think what spirit dwells within thee:
Think what the Father's smiles are thine:
Think what Jesus did to win thee;
Child of heaven, can'st thou repine? ......

With these thoughts and the feelings that God and the Christ were with me, I felt hopeful. I remembered the audio bible on my smart phone. I plugged it in and placed earphones in my ears and listened to the bible until I fell asleep. I think I had been asleep for more than 4 hours when I was woken up by a strong voice of encouragement and direction, 'What are you waiting for? You are already healed. Let go and be you, perfect and whole.' I know that voice, I have heard it before through His angels, I thought to myself. I almost jumped out of bed and ran away. 'Where would you go? Look at you, you cannot even walk let alone run.' I found my inner voice saying. That discouraging voice again!!!! That was my own thinking, it could only be mine. I managed to say thank you then went back to sleep. This time a deep sleep, from about 1:30am to about 6:00am. I slept as though I had been drugged. This was a good sign.

No looking back

Two weeks after the Lord spoke to me, I was walking much better than before. I started smiling again, everyone around me began to see the change. My daughter, always by my side every minute she was allowed in hospital was now the little angel feeding me spiritually as well as materially, bringing me food from lunch to tea. She also started to research on what dietary changes I could make that would aid my recovery. She told me to cut off sugar as soon as possible and stopped serving me meat. All the dairy products also disappeared. I started gaining energy and walking about. I was grateful and held on to the garment of the living God. I clung on as if there was nothing else to do.

The Traditional Marriage

To be honest, even if one sees progress in one's life, there is always a trace of doubt buried inside, they say it's human nature. I was still toying with the idea of taking my life. I really did not want to be a burden to anyone, especially my kids. 'There must be a way to leave this universe quietly' I thought to myself. I lay there in the hospital bed sketching and scheming my own death. If my daughter got married to her fiancé, Gareth, of 5 years, then she could be a mother to my son when I was gone. It could be the best answer for all involved. I started probing her for her intentions. I knew they loved each other, they were best of friends, which I feel is a great foundation for a relationship. And after all, Maureen, Gareth's mum had become like a sister to me. She would be there for them. What a great plan. I approached her very gently and encouraged her to think about it and to feel free to go ahead since they had been planning it for a long time even before I got sick. I said to her 'I will be happy to have a gift of your marriage as my new-birth gift. That will be the icing on the cake of a new world for me'. At first, she did not feel that it was a good idea but with a little nagging, she agreed, thinking she would be helping me in my healing process!

Everything was arranged quickly, and the date was set. My ex-husband, who also used to come and visit me in hospital, got involved in the plans. He was concerned about it, but I reassured him that it was for the best of all the concerned parties. I was inwardly excited knowing that the end of my suffering is coming. If only they knew. Maureen was fitting well in the position of being their mother, she was there most of the time supporting them and counselling them. She was very good and cooked organic food for me every time; it was a perfect fit.

The day of the marriage came. I convinced the Doctors to let me go home on the Friday even against their own advice; my temperature was up and down like mad. I promised them, the docs that if I felt any change I would rush back, especially since I would be just ten minutes away from the hospital. I remember clearly the sequence of events on this Friday afternoon; getting home, people coming in to help. My cousins, my aunts, my nieces and the whole lot of the community came to rally behind us. What a day! I remember sitting on my leather seat, seeing people busy unselfishly helping to make the day a success and thinking how wonderful God is. I was in pain but kept a brave face for the occasion because I wanted it to proceed so badly. Having a strong family or community support system is amazing. Everyone was giving their all to make it a success. I watched and listened hopelessly from my lounge not being able to do a thing. Oh! If only they could tell that I was planning my own death. I was really happy, my own joy, a feeling of achievement that things were falling into place just as I wanted them.

Figure 2: Me and my Daughter after my healing

God's plans are not man's plans; neither are his thoughts my thoughts. All my plans and thoughts came to nothing because of the love and support of family, friends and Christian Science Practitioners who were always praying from a distance. My secondary school friend, who lives in South Africa was also on the case.

Yes, I went back into hospital worse than I had been before I came home for the wedding, but I was so happy that things were going to be great now.

CHAPTER 5

How did the journey out of the hole begin?

Being a Christian Scientist – I love being one – made me believe that all I ever needed was spiritual food, nothing else. I think I took the verse 'Man shall not live by bread,' Matthew 4:4, but left 'alone' out of the context. In full, the verse says 'Man shall not live by bread alone, but by every word that proceedeth out of the mouth of God' It meant that men shall eat bread but cannot forget to feed their spiritual being. During these days, I had the time to look at what the wise book had to say about food. In Genesis 1:29 "And God said, Behold, I have given you every herb bearing seed, which is upon the face of all the earth, and every tree, in the which is the fruit of a tree yielding seed; to you it shall be for meat" Even all the animals were commissioned to eat the grass. It became clear to me that at the beginning God created everything else; he gave us herbs of the field to be meat to us. Living a spiritual life means adhering to the word of God in its entirety. I learnt that my spiritual man, my inner man does not have anything to do with the box, the temple which is my body. The box needs washing up, feeding and loving. It is like a car; the engine needs some TLC every now and then. The car needs fuel, petrol or diesel or now electricity in order to move about. The body needs water, some natural herbs, greens and fruits to keep it functioning properly. My spirit man remains undisturbed as long as it gets spiritual nourishment, the word of God and my body, herbs. This led me to the beginning of the end.

My first call of action

My journey started really when I was still in the hospital ward when I stopped eating sugar and meat. During her research, my daughter had relied on the help of Sister Mary Matambanadzo, who found a Doctor, Dr Matanda who is a Christian. He gave my daughter a long list of what the Bible says about food. He encouraged me not to eat sugar or meat. He encouraged me to eat plant-based foods and a lot of fruits and pulses. The nurses or Health assistants would give me sugar for my tea and biscuits, but I would not touch them because I had been advised that the cancer, I was fighting loved it. I started having black tea without sugar, no milk at all. I also drank lots of water. I would drink about 4 litres of water per day and even right through the night. It was difficult going to the toilet constantly, but it had to be done. When I moved into the side room (to die), they had to place a commode pan by the bed. I started wearing incontinence pads which still were not enough to contain all the urine. I would use the commode but still need to have my pads changed. I knew I had to dig deeper into myself otherwise it was game over.

Isaiah 66:13 "As one whom his mother comforteth, so will I comfort you".

This is a verse from the bible which had started speaking to me as I was reading the bible and would come to me so often throughout the day. I felt comforted and encouraged knowing that I was not alone. My joy did not last long as it became clear in my thoughts that my mother left me when I was very young so which mother was comforting me, how would God comfort me? The peace which had awakened in me quickly vanished and I began to cry, tears just started running down my cheeks and I could not control them. I was trying hard to feel that love from God, but it seemed like it was out of reach. I forced myself to continue searching the scriptures.

This verse spoke to me again;

Psalms 107: 6-7 'Then they cried to the Lord in their trouble, and he delivered them from distresses. And He led them forth by the right way, that they might go to a city of habitation'

20 'He sent forth his word and healed them, and delivered them from their destructions'

21 'Oh that men would praise his goodness, and for his wonderful works to the children of men!'

Wow, these verses jerked me back to who I really am; the image and likeness of the Most High God. I have always believed that my God was my mother, always there for me and always knowing my need for him. He knows me and cares for me. All the challenges I had faced before came to surface. I saw myself 20 years ago when I was told that I was going to use antibiotics the rest of my life, for disease of the bones, taking 2 tablets three times a day but the day I came out of hospital I had challenged myself and vowed never to take anything the Doctors say seriously because they do not know me. I believed that God is my only healer and yes, I received my healing after throwing all the tablets in the bin, never to suffer again.

As I continued to study a lot more encouraging verses came forth.

Psalm 17:7-9 "Shew thy marvelous loving kindness, O thou that savest by thy right hand them which put their trust in thee from those that rise up against them. Keep me as the apple of the eye, hide me under the shadow of thy wings. From the wicked that oppress me, from my deadly enemies who compass me about".

I was beginning to trust God again as my Father/Mother. His fatherhood is expressed in protection, provision, wisdom and guidance. I surrendered all to him and trusted that whatever I have to do from now on has to be God-led. I placed my hand in His (spiritual) and that firm grip reassured me. His motherhood which is found in tenderness, attentiveness, comfort and love embraced me unconditionally. Everyone coming to me from then on, I began to see them expressing these qualities. Most of them were very tender in giving care and attention to detail because otherwise both of us would be in danger. They made sure I was comfortable, and they expressed so much love that I felt that yes indeed, I was 'The apple of the eye.' The eyeball, or globe of the eye, the pupil, is called the apple because of the shape but also because of its great value. It's so valuable it is carefully protected by the eyelids that automatically close when there is the least possibility of danger. It is the emblem of that which was most precious and jealously protected (biblestudytools.com). I felt that love and trusted it so much that I surrendered all my power into holding on to His unconditional love.

Holding on

As I journeyed through with my studies, the Psalms were always reassuring, and they spoke directly to my soul. Psalms 139:1-3 "O Lord thou hast searched me and known me. Thou knowest my down sitting and mine uprising, thou understandeth my thought afar off. Thou compasseth my path and my lying down, and art acquainted with all my ways". "Oh my God", I thought to myself, "whilst I am lying here thinking the doctors are going to figure out how to heal me, God knows all about me and disease and sickness are not part of it. He knows what goes in my mind when I am asleep, the dreams I have and my hopes for tomorrow. He knows what the doctors were going to do to me but one thing I love about him, he gave me a choice; choice to follow him or man and man's creations, to choose life or death, to choose love or sorrow". I knew I was waging war with opposition but as always, I looked forward to winning.

I decided to argue on the side of health and harmony. I felt at peace as I let go of the need to want to understand or reason about the next move or step. I knew beyond doubt that God alone was the source of my being and as per his promise, He would never leave me nor forsake me. No matter how I was feeling, my condition to the human eye or per my own feelings, my bond with him was intact. So never leaving harmony or returning to it because it has been there all the time no matter what condition I seemed to be in, there was, and would never be a lapse from harmony. It brought back a lot of memories of how the people of old won their wars or challenges. In the Old Testament, after Joshua took over from Moses, he trusted God to the last core of his being, he followed the law and never turned from it at any juncture. They walked on dry ground whilst crossing the Jordan River and nobody was hurt or was caught up in the challenge. They did not have doctors to tell them how to survive or to see to their health, but they trusted God for 40 years. They depended on reading the book of the law every day, regardless. They reminded each other how Moses led their forefathers to cross the Red Sea with Pharaoh pursuing them. Joshua and the priests asked the children to sanctify themselves, they needed to confess their oneness with God, to cleanse themselves of the dust from their journey around the wilderness and start afresh, with a clean outlook and be sure that God was their strength and help.

Joshua 3:16 "And as they that bore the ark were come unto Jordan, and the feet of the priests that bore the ark were dipped in the brim of the water, (for Jordan overfloweth all his banks all the time of harvest)". The Priests stepped into the water, the waters parted, receded and so stood on dry ground. The people passed on dry ground to the last man. This does not mean there was no opposition, no challenges. Many people from within the camp were in doubt, they did not go.

Those who did not want to be sanctified did not cross over, they were left behind and ended up dying in the wilderness. The picture became clearer to me thinking of the story, I had to trust what the word of God, my creator, said about me. I was at that place in my life where I could put my hand in God's and walk without any problem. The challenging Jordan was in front of me and it did not look good, but His word and promises were sufficient for me. I had to stand in the gap for my own healing and I knew I had my priests scattered around the world holding spiritual hands for me. It felt like I had to walk over the dry land to the other side no matter what the material sense was seeing.

I have a relatively big family and most of them are in the medical field. They urged me to work with the doctors and just do as told. Mary Baker Eddy in her art of writing, Science and Health With Key to the Scriptures, had taught me to know the truth about who I am before God and trust His word/truth about me. She brought the Bible alive into my life. She wrote in, Science & Health 180.25-27 "When man is governed by God, the ever-present Mind who understands all things, man knows that with God all things are possible". After reading this, I began to challenge my trust in God, my oneness with Mother-love but only for a short time for I knew I did not have anybody who cares for me like God has always done and is always doing. Yes, my mother passed on when I was young, but her love was equal to no one who ever offered to be a mother to my siblings and me. I began to remember how she fed me, washed me, teaching me to be a good girl, teaching me to love other fellow human beings. In that moment I felt her presence and warmth covering me, I could smell her as if she was still with us. I knew God was asking me to renew my love for him and his promises for me again.

As I continued to do my studies with my daughter, we came to discover that thought is like fluid, moving every time, it was like one minute I see and feel the love of God then the next minute I felt like I did not have any choice but to let go. The word of God was the ground I was standing on and the minute I let negative thoughts into my mind, things would start to go bad. I started listening to my bible books every time using my mobile and that would encourage me. Singing hymns and praising God for His mercies became an everyday ritual.

My brother was always encouraging me to follow the directions the doctors were telling me. He knew nothing else but the pharmaceuticals. I knew he doubted me and my walk with God, but I knew it was from a good place, love, though there were some elements of fear too. I did not want to let the lack of faith disturb or bother me. Like most of the time people get in the story of their own challenges while others interfere with the healing process which stops or slows down the healing. It was my brother's own story which he had written about me, and so did many others but it was not my own, so I did not need to believe it. I knew and believed that God governed, guarded and guided my life and everyone else's worry was their human stories and so did not bother me. The 3Gs were my pillar now. Just as Joshua agreed when Moses gave him the mantle, I felt the need to accept and take responsibility of my life and sacrifice whatever was holding me back and turn the theory into practice, walking only in the practical road to holiness. I knew that I needed to take the law of God everywhere with me, my thoughts and my dealings, and that my progress will make it possible to bless others and help everyone I will meet or whom I come across, to learn also to put the theory of God's word into practice.

True Security - Unconditional love

Most of us know the story of the Hebrew boys, in a foreign land where their every movement/action was guarded all the time. What they ate was under scrutiny and their association also was under guard. Yes, I felt like that especially when I could not eat or walk on my own. The 4 boys believed beyond unbelief that God sustained them. They knew without doubt that no man who was created by God could touch or harm them in any way. They knew they were covered by God's love and that they also had each other for support and encouragement. They knew that they were in the palm of His hand and that no matter what, God was there for them. My daughter's continuous presence on my side reminded me of God's unconditional love. Because of this, I was not afraid that something was going to happen but stayed in the panoply of His love. I started feeling the love from those around me including the doctors, nurses and even cleaners. Everybody was smiling and chatting with me. I knew my daughter could not be with me every minute, but whenever possible she was there. My son was very supportive and tried being there as much as he could but could not always stomach the pain and the person his mom had turned to be. He had never seen me in that state so being the youngest he chose to do all the running around. He did all the chores for his sister and me but sitting by my side for a long time was too painful for him.

It was such an amazing journey when people had to give up their time to come and be by my side. Some came from as far as South Africa, Faith and her dad Brian who never stopped praying every day. My cousin and friend, Kennedy Makwenda, came to visit me with his wife and 3 children even though they had very little time to be together, since the wife and children live in Zimbabwe. It was just selfless, and I hope and trust God that I will be able to do that for other people, the whole wide world.

CHAPTER 6

Leaving Hospital

After 8 months of living in and out of the oncology ward, the day finally came when I was told I could stay at home but to come back as soon as I feel anything challenging. I did not have to go through the process of registering again but could go straight to the ward. They also emphasised that I must stay indoors and avoid congested places in town otherwise I would get infected especially since my immune system had been destroyed and my body could not fight against any diseases in a natural way. This was one of the red warning signs; it was like I was told that I needed to rebuild my own immune system. I thought about all the toxins which they had fed me with and wondered how we could do this; Samantha and I had now become a team on researching on what was good for me. We embarked on a marathon race of detoxifying my whole system. What was there to help remove the poison which was embedded in my body and my thoughts as well?

Detoxification: Ways Which Can Be Employed

Detoxification is defined as the purification of the body system from unwanted materials. It involves the processes of neutralizing and eliminating unwanted substances from the body of living organism. Living organisms are constantly exposed to toxic materials which are either generated in their body system as a result of metabolic activities or present in the environment they inhabited. These harmful substances, which retarded the proper body functions, originated from a variety of sources such as chemical (e.g. environmental pollutants, insecticides, food preservatives etc.); biological (microorganisms e.g. bacteria and fungi; allergen), physical (ionizing radiation).

These harmful substances are known to be the basis of diseases and poor health state of the body. To cope with these problems, the body is equipped with some organs such as liver, kidney, and colon which work together to get rid of these substances. Also, some mechanisms are put in place to eliminate these toxic substances. The excessive bombardment of the body by these toxins overwhelms the body's protective ability and leads to improper functioning of the body. At this stage, there is a need to employ means that could effectively detoxify these toxins.

Ways to Detoxify Body from Toxins

There are several ways that can be employed for the effective detoxification of the body system. The popular among these are:

- Consumption of organic foods
- Drinking a lot of water
- Eating more fibre in its most natural form
- Engaging in yoga for a new type of exercise and meditation
- Avoid alcohol consumption and cigarette smoking
- Avoid junk foods, preserved foods and sugar
- Avoid obvious environmental toxins
- Avoid strenuous activity
- Fasting
- Increase circulation by massaging pressure points and skin brushing

- Replacing a meal each day with a detoxifying smoothie

The above stated detoxification practices promote healthy function of the body. Moreover, other benefits that can be derived from the detoxification processes include:

(i) Boost of body energy

(ii) Help ridding the body of excess waste

(iii)   Help with weight Loss

(iv)   Boost of body's immune system

(v) Slowdown of the ageing process

Foods suitable for Detoxification

Several practices are available for healthy detoxification of numerous unwanted substances that are generated within the body system or entered the body from external environment. The famous among these practices is diet detoxification. Diet detoxification entails the consumption of fresh, natural food substances that provide the body with all nutrients required for the efficient body function and withdrawal of food substances that poses threat to the body. A good diet detoxifier supports healthy weight loss, boosts body immune system, maintains normal body growth, mops off free radicals generated in the body and also helps in eliminating waste products from the body. There are a lot of food substances which are exemplary for detoxification practices. The best of these food substances are those produced from organic farming which includes grains, fruits and vegetables. These food substances are devoid of any artificial means of preservation and processing, and are either consumed raw or prepared as smoothies. Below is the list of some food substances that I have found effective for detoxification practices.

- Fruits
    - Citrus fruits (Grape, Orange, Tangerine etc.)
    - Berries
    - Apples
    - Avocado
    - Banana
    - Pineapple

- Vegetables
    - Green leafy vegetables
        - Cabbage
        - Lentils
        - Broccoli

- Kale
- spinach

Non leafy vegetables

- Garlic and Onions
- Cucumber
- Carrot

- Grains
  - Oat
  - Rice etc.

Others include:
- Green Tea
- Artichokes
- Beets
- Milk thistle
- Wheat grass
- Fennel
- Ginger
- Olive oil
- Beans
- Nuts and Seeds.
- Yoghurt etc.

These food substances consist of enzymes, vitamins, mineral elements, fibres, phytochemicals etc. that helps in maintaining good health of the body. Fruits such as citrus, pineapple and apple are good sources of vitamin C which is a potent antioxidant capable of neutralizing the effect of free radicals and reactive species. Moreover, grapes contain resveratrol, which can protect the body against cancer and diabetes, and potentially prevent blood clots. The brilliant colour of some fruits such as carrots are as a result of the presence of important molecules including vitamin A, flavonoids, lycopenes, carotene. These compounds are potent antioxidants.

Vegetables, grains, beans and some other fruits are good sources of fibre which promotes the healthy function of some organs such as heart, colon, kidney, liver etc.

However, these food substances can also be prepared in the form of smoothies by blending the raw fruit or vegetable with other ingredients such as water, ice, dairy products or sweeteners. Smoothies are usually preferred to juice in the detoxification practices because juice contains only the extractable liquid from the fruits or vegetables, whereas smoothies consist of all edible parts of the food including the pulp, and as such, contain many more important molecules than juice. The following smoothies are important for detoxifying purposes:

- ⬚ Creamy Cranberry Vanilla Smoothie
- ⬚ Banana pineapple green drink
- ⬚ French toast smoothies
- ⬚ Berry Oat Smoothie
- ⬚ Vegan Detox Green Monster Smoothie
- ⬚ Banana Peach Almond Smoothie
- ⬚ Apple Pie Smoothie
- ⬚ Green Orange Dreamsicle Smoothie
- ⬚ Grapefruit Smoothie
- ⬚ Ginger and Peach Green Smoothie
- ⬚ Blueberry Peachy Lemon Smoothies

Detoxification the natural way

Most of the methods we found started by encouraging taking a lot of water. I would drink about 5 litres of water per day. As you can imagine, you will be going to the toilet more frequently. I started drinking green tea and stopped all the dairy products which meant no milk in my tea because I learnt that the cows, we use for our milk were fed with a lot of chemicals. I stopped eating sugar and learnt to drink tea without it. Lemons were introduced in my diet as well. I went on a week of having smoothies only. I went away for a few days and carried 6 bottles of ready-made smoothies and was drinking loads of water.

CHAPTER 7

Studies

Here are some of the studies/research which were done by a few individuals who showed me a better way of doing things and all this was written and researched by Chris Wark who healed himself from cancer too.

Here is an excerpt from the papers abstract:

'The extracts from cruciferous vegetables as well as those from vegetables of the genus Allium inhibited the proliferation of all tested cancer cell lines whereas extracts from vegetables most commonly consumed in Western countries were much less effective. The antiproliferative effect of vegetables was specific to cells of cancerous origin and was found to be largely independent of their antioxidant properties. These results thus indicate that vegetables have very different inhibitory activities towards cancer cells and that the inclusion of cruciferous and Allium vegetables

in the diet is essential for effective dietary-based chemo preventive strategies.'

Translation:

- ☐ Allium and cruciferous veggies stopped cancer cell growth.
- ☐ Commonly consumed vegetables did not work as well.
- ☐ The antioxidant content of veggies was not a key anti-cancer factor.
- ☐ Different vegetables work for different cancers.
- ☐ Allium and <u>cruciferous</u> veggies should be eaten to prevent cancer.

So the most commonly consumed vegetables in Western countries had very little effect on cancer cell growth.

The top three (potatoes, lettuce, and carrots) account for 60% of the vegetables we Westerners are eating. 32% of our vegetable intake is potatoes, and half of that is actually French fries. Nice.

Dark greens, cruciferous veggies, and garlic account for less than 1% of our Western diet! Hello?

An interesting note:

Radishes were found to stop tumour growth by 95-100% for breast and stomach cancer but may have even increased tumour growth by 20-25% in pancreatic, brain, lung and kidney cancer. Definitely something to keep in mind.

Before You Write Off the 'Poor Performers'

It's important to keep in mind that this is a laboratory study showing only what a vegetable extract did to someone when applied directly to cancer cells.

The study does not take into account the vitamins, minerals, and phytonutrients that indirectly support your body's ability to repair, regenerate, detoxify, and heal.

Cancer is a product of a toxic body, so detoxing your body is critical in healing cancer.

For example, carrots are a potent source of beta-carotene, which is converted to Vitamin A in the body. Vitamin A supports your liver. Your liver is a critical component of your immune system because it detoxifies your body.

Having said all that, it makes sense to focus on eating tons of the veggies that were actually killing cancer in the lab.

Also, this study confirms why what I did in 2004 worked.

I ate copious amounts of these cancer-fighting vegetables every day in my Giant Cancer-Fighting Salad, specifically spinach, kale, broccoli, cauliflower, onions, red cabbage, and garlic powder. I had no idea about leeks or else they would have been in there, too.

Garlic is an Anti-Cancer Vegetable

And I ate several close of garlic per day.

So, I would just crush up the cloves and swallow them with a mouthful of water.

I also took Kyolic Garlic Extract.

And yes, I reeked. But I lived to tell the tale!

Top 10 Anti-Cancer Vegetables

1. Garlic
2. Leeks
3. Yellow and Green Onions
4. Broccoli
5. Brussels Sprouts
6. Cauliflower
7. Kale
8. Red Cabbage and Curly Cabbage
9. Spinach
10. Beet Root

Honourable Mentions:

1. Asparagus
2. Fiddlehead
3. Green beans
4. Radishes

By Sayer Ji - Originally published on Greenmed.info

There is a medicinal spice so timelessly interwoven with the origins of human culture and metabolism, so thoroughly supported by modern scientific inquiry, as to be unparalleled in its proven value to human health and well-being.

Indeed, turmeric turns the entire drug-based medical model on its head.

Instead of causing far more side effects than therapeutic ones, as is the case for most patented pharmaceutical medications, turmeric possesses hundreds of potential *side benefits* — having been empirically demonstrated to positively modulate over 160 different physiological pathways in the mammalian body.

While no food or herb is right for everyone, and everything has the potential for unintended, adverse side effects, turmeric is truly unique in its exceptionally high margin of safety vis-à-vis the drugs it has been compared with, e.g. hydrocortisone, ibuprofen, chemotherapy agents.

Furthermore, nothing within the modern-day pharmaceutical armamentarium comes even remotely close to turmeric's *6,000-year track record of safe use in Ayurvedic medicine.*

Why Turmeric Will Likely Never Be FDA (Food and Drug Administration) [3]Approved

Despite its vast potential for alleviating human suffering, turmeric will likely never receive the FDA stamp of approval, due to its lack of exclusivity, patentability and therefore profitability.

Truth be told, the FDA's 'gold standard' for proving the value of a prospective medicinal substance betrays the age-old aphorism: 'he who owns the gold makes the rules,' and unless an investor is willing to risk losing the 800+ million dollars that must be spent upfront, the FDA-required multi-phased double-blind, randomized clinical trials will not occur.

---

[3] USA food and drug administration: www.fda.gov

All the Incredible Turmeric Benefits

At GreenMedInfo.com, we have reviewed over 5,000 study abstracts from the National Library of Medicine's bibliographic database known as MEDLINE and have discovered over 600 potential health benefits of turmeric, and/or its primary polyphenol known as curcumin.

These can be viewed on our turmeric research page which is dedicated to disseminating the research on the topic to a larger audience.

Some of the most amazing demonstrated properties of turmeric and/or curcumin include these turmeric benefits:

- Destroying Multi-Drug Resistant Cancer
- Destroying Cancer Stem Cells (arguably, the root of all cancer)
- Protecting Against Radiation-Induced Damage
- Reducing Unhealthy Levels of Inflammation
- Protecting Against Heavy Metal Toxicity

- Preventing and Reversing Alzheimer's Disease Associated Pathologies

Again, what is so amazing is not that turmeric may have value in *dozens of health conditions simultaneously*, or that it may improve conditions that are completely resistant to conventional treatment, but that there are over **six hundred additional health conditions** it may also be valuable in preventing and/or treating.

Consider also the fact that turmeric grows freely on the Earth, and you will understand why its very existence threatens billions of dollars in pharmaceutical industry revenue.

Important Note from Ocean Robbins, Food Revolution Network CEO:

Many of our members have been asking how much curcumin to take, how to take it in a bioavailable form, and where to get curcumin from a source they can trust. The challenge with taking full advantage of the curcumin in turmeric is low bioavailability. Personally, I love mixing

*fresh and dried turmeric into all sorts of foods —
and I always try to include black pepper with it
because studies show that piperine (found in
black pepper) helps increase absorbability.*

*But now PuraTHRIVE has developed a curcumin
supplement that utilizes a cutting-edge micelle
liposomal delivery mechanism that's been found
to* **increase bioavailability by up to 185 times**.
*Their formula also contains ginger oil, vegan
DHA fatty acids from algae, and beneficial
phospholipids. The product is* **100% vegan,
organic, soy-free, and non-GMO**.

Thank you, Chris, for opening my eyes and just
knowing that what I was doing was never far
from what other people have done. There are so
many other studies which showed me the light
and Ty Bollinger is one of them. He is doing what
he is doing because he lost a number of family
members to cancer so now his desire is to educate
as many people as he could possibly do which is
the main reason that also drove me to write this
book and share with others what I did in small
doses.

I am not writing what I did in detail because I felt it will be lost in the story, so writing an e-book seemed more appropriate. I will also offer a one-on-one coaching or rather just sharing my journey more intimately.

CHAPTER 8

How I ended up being in the Queen Elizabeth Hospital

Quantum Hearts

After being home for a few months, I was discharged at the beginning of January and enjoyed time working on my nutrition and spiritual life. It was so funny when after being home for a day I started checking my emails and Face Book to see what I had missed during my wilderness period. I saw messages from 1 year ago which I had never managed to read which were really helpful, people who had heard that I was not well had been reaching out and praying for me. How beautiful the world of computers has changed the universe and made it so small. I quickly replied to some people, and others called me when they knew I was home. I was humbled to hear how they had been thinking about me and that our God, the Creator of all, had a mission for me. I just sank into that and spent more time reading the bible and praying.

Now that I was home, a lot of people could come to visit and now I could use my laptop instead of depending on the mobile handset. I was so surprised during this time to find Jean Houston's email in my inbox and she was offering a course and the following day was the closing day. I had read and followed her for some time and honestly enjoyed reading and doing some of her exercises. At seeing this email, a surge of joy and urgency pushed me into signing up for it. I had not been dealing with my finances but fortunately just that morning my daughter had brought back my card and showed me what was left in the bank. It was not much but I urgently took out my card and filled out the form. It was five hundred pounds well spent. I am ever so grateful I did that.

I signed up on a Tuesday and on that Thursday, I was scheduled to go into hospital to have a check-up, which could have ended up being a surgery, for some ulcerations which had developed on my anus. Just before we left home, I found out that I had some videos from Jean Houston, so I took those and my laptop and watched them when I was at the hospital. It helped me so much because

I did not spend time feeling sorry for myself and getting stressed seeing a lot of my fellow patients groaning in pain. This was at a different hospital, so I had to stay in my room since I did not know anywhere to go. That was an amazing video which sort of opened me more to what I was going to expect.

After all the check-ups and consultations, I was given some cream and sent home to use it then come back after two weeks to see if there was any need for an operation. This was God-given time because I started the online course same time as the others. It was so wonderful to see how people who never met and most likely will never meet, quickly got involved in each other's affairs. We would listen to Jean talking and sharing with us how powerful God the Creator was and that we have all these things at our disposal. She encouraged us to form some online community and suggested that we should meet once a week before our next meeting with her. This was an amazing opportunity to work with others and help/support each other. That is when the group Quantum Hearts was started.

When I went home from the hospital, in January, I could hardly sit in the lounge, was always in bed and to be fair it was good for my children because they could just feed me and go on with their lives leaving me to entertain myself. My bedroom was very close to the bathroom and I had a commode chair I could use if needed plus I was now receiving some incontinent pads which helped a lot, because they came to my aid. I started having these meetings from the comfort of my bed, not by choice but by design. I could hardly sit up, so most of the time I just laid in bed and during these times of online meetings, I just propped myself up and shared with others. I had lost my hair and my niece Lucille came to give her cousins a break and wisely when she knew that I had gone bald, brought a wig which really helped me a lot to be able to look at myself in the mirror. With the Quantum Hearts I never wore a wig because I wanted to be me in my normal environment.

I am ever so grateful to this bunch of people, some I have met in person and we have become close friends but others we still communicate once in a while in Face Book. I have met Nancy Jean Mirales, Sarah Caddick, Rita Murray, Dil, Ursula Kirn-Defferary, Susane Schneider, Maureen Dickie, Judith Costa, Eileen Murray, Aryn Rose, Dil Light, Ida Rump, Jolita Tolkko,

Susan Miners, Sandi Hughes, Rosalind Dunwell, Jeanne Dockins, Enrique Morales, Jacqueline Tellis, Rocco Caratozzolo, Rakael Hava, Gillian Nutt, Sarah Gill, Julie Bloomer, Mary Spain, Birgit Spies, Helen Young, Mel Brownie and many more whose names I did not mention. The Universe gave you permission to be part of my life and I am so blessed to have met you at my weakest moment. I LOVE, I LOVE, I LOVE YOU all. You taught me to meditate, quieten the mind and feel God in action; you helped me learn how to love me and allow Jesus Christ, who is my friend, my healer, to be part of my life. We played together and some of us met up one day in London and were hugging trees for the better part of the day.

I also met my brother, Brian Ian Richard Calder, who is Nancy Mirales' husband, one of the Quantum Hearts sisters. He introduced me to a wonderful nutrient which helped me get the energy I needed to start living my life. You were prepared to go an extra mile with me, visiting me with Nancy and meeting up for coffee. You are so cool brother and I love you so much. Let's continue to rock the world.

It was after going through the exercises that I regained my voice, went back to the hospital in April for a random check-up, and the doctors said that I still have some cancer cells left and needed to either have surgery or radio therapy. I was shocked when they said if I do not do that I will die. I was upset at first but managed to remember who I am so that I pulled myself up and lived in the present moment, and restarted my journey back into my understanding of who I am. I had to also do a lot of meditation to help me anchor myself into the most beautiful being.

CHAPTER 9

Cancer

Types and Causes of Cancer

Cancer is a disease condition characterized by an uncontrolled growth of abnormal cells that result in the production of populations of cells which have acquired the ability to multiply and invade the host's surrounding tissue and distant tissues. Cancer cells often begin as a tumour and are then promoted by mutation to form a benign tumour which later progresses to a malignant tumour that metastasises (spreads) and affects the distant tissues and cells. This invasive feature poses lethal threat to normal host cells. Cancer is one of the leading killer diseases in the world, which has accounted for more than a million deaths annually. Cancer often arises from the mutation (sudden change in the structure of DNA) of the critical genes (Proto-oncogenes and Tumour-suppressor genes) which play a notable role in cell division.

Classification of Cancer

Cancers are classified based on the type of cells the tumour cells resemble, and those cells are presumed to be the origin of the tumour. The following are the major classes of cancer.

- carcinoma
- sarcoma
- lymphoma and leukaemia

Carcinoma

Carcinoma is a type of cancer that develops from the epithelial cells. Epithelia cells form layer in outer surface of the body and also in most internal organs where they perform vital functions necessary for the survival of the organisms. Carcinoma is the most common type of cancer representing about 80-90% of all known types of cancer. Examples of cancers in this group include liver cancer, breast cancer, prostate cancer, lung cancer and colon cancer.

Sarcoma

This is a type of malignant tumour that affects connective tissues such as bones, cartilages, fats and nerves. Sarcomas, which are a less common type of cancer include iomyosarcoma, liposarcoma and osteosarcoma

Lymphoma **and** Leukaemia

These are cancers affecting blood-forming cells. While *lymphomas* affect the lymphatic system, leukemia affects mainly the white blood cells.

Others classes of cancer include: Germ cell tumor and Blastoma.

Agents Known to Cause Cancer

The agents known to cause cancer are termed carcinogens. Carcinogens combine directly or indirectly with the DNA molecules and this results in mutation. The inability of the cell to repair the damage, and subsequent attack of these mutated cells causes cancer. The major carcinogens include:

Viruses (hepatitis B, hepatitis C and human papillomavirus)

Ionizing radiations (e.g X-ray and gamma rays)

Exposure to radiation may lead to the disruption of the structure of DNA bases and result in mutation. The inability of the cell to repair this damage may further progress to cancer.

Chemicals

More than 500 chemical carcinogens have been documented. The major groups of chemical carcinogens include:

(i) Aromatic amines e.g. 4- amino bipheny

(ii) Halogenated Hydrocarbon e.g. poly vinyl chloride

(iii) Polycyclic Aromatic Hydrocarbon e.g. benzo[a]pyrene

(iv) Nitrosamines

Most of these chemicals especially the aromatic compounds resemble DNA bases and can intercalate into the DNA structure, forming a permanent structure. Thus, chemical carcinogens can either combine directly with the DNA bases or metabolize into an active metabolite that produces damaging effects to the DNA structure.

Aflatoxins are naturally occurring chemical carcinogens produced by certain fungi that grow on food crops such as grains, nuts and peanut butter. Consumption of such foods infested with these fungi can predispose the body to cancer. Several food preservatives used such as sodium benzoate and nitrites have also proven to be carcinogenic. Tobacco smoke consists of several chemicals including benzopyrene and nitrosamine that are potent carcinogens. Moreover, activities such as overheating and charring of food particles can lead to the formation of minute compounds that are carcinogenic.

Aside from these agents that cause cancer, certain lifestyle factors (diet, physical activity, and alcohol consumption) and environmental factors contribute to the formation of cancer through mutation of the critical genes.

WAYS TO DETOXIFY BODY FROM TOXINS

There are several ways that can be employed for the effective detoxification of the body system. The popular among these are:

i.   Consumption of organic foods

ii.   Drinking a lot of water

iii. Eating more fiber in its most natural form

iv. Yoga

v. Avoiding alcohol consumption and cigarette smoking

vi. Avoiding junk foods, preserved foods, and sugar

vii. Avoiding obvious environmental toxins

viii. Avoiding strenuous physical activity

ix. Fasting

x. Increase circulation by massaging pressure points and skin brushing

xi. Replacing a meal each day with a detoxifying smoothie

The above-stated detoxification exercises promote healthy function of the body. Moreover, other benefits that can be derived from the detoxification processes include:

i.   Boosting of body energy

ii.   Help to rid the body of excess waste

iii.   Help with Weight Loss

iv.   The boost of the body's immune system

v.   Slow down of the aging process

What I did most of the time

1) I would wake up and drink 2 litres of water with a few slices of lemon on an empty stomach to detoxify before eating anything then make smoothie.

One example of types of smoothie is: 2 tbsp of chia seed, 1 cup almond milk and 1 tbsp of moringa and half a cup of blueberries and about 5 medium sized strawberries and blend together. I would have green salad about 2 times and 'sadza', thick porridge twice a day with green vegetables and kidney beans

2) I had started worrying so much that committing suicide was becoming food for thought every day but when

someone introduced me to meditation, I felt blessed and relieved. I used to meditate for 15 minutes every morning, what we Christians call silent prayer. This helped me in staying focused on who I knew God created me to be.

3)I created a black bin bag where I would place all my worries and concerns. I would visualise putting those worries or sometimes write letters to God or to myself and burn them or throw them in the black bag. This really helped me because I felt like I was doing something about my situation not just laying in bed or thinking that if I could drink some jik which was in my bathroom I would be free from suffering

4) I was introduced to drinking warm ribena and a lot of green tea which has now become my norm. I never liked coffee because of the caffeine and since I had stopped taking sugar it tasted horrible. My taste buds said no to the sharp taste.

5) I had always wanted to write a book, so I started writing things which were

nagging me to death. I started to write any negative thought in an opposite way, if I felt like killing myself, I started loving myself and seeing myself doing great things. At one point I saw myself standing in front of a large crowd sharing my story of healing and it made me want to do that and so I am now a public speaker.

6) Walking and exercise - I really found value in taking a walk every day along the canal, because I lived near one, or just walking up and down in my garden. It all worked well because it gave me a reason of waking up every morning.

CHAPTER 10

Inspirational Quotes from different people and the Bible

Mary Baker Eddy, ''No and Yes.39. True prayer is not asking God for love, it is learning to love, and to include all mankind in one affection. Prayer is the utilization of the love wherewith He loves us''

Remember there is no such thing as a small act of kindness. Every act creates a ripple with no logical end.

The mind sees itself in infinite expression as an idea- sees it within itself.

-absolutely impossible for man- God's idea, to exist outside the realm of infinite Mind, of Divine Love, endless Life, and perpetual harmony

The idea of Spirit is instantly available, always distinct, individual, perfect, eternal

The idea is spiritual and complete, Man's whole is what God knows of Himself, it lacks nothing.

The Master always had all that was needed when it was needed- health for the sick, loaves for the multitudes, money for taxes, compassion for the world

How do we find our centre, by realising our oneness with the infinite Power, God, Principal, Love, Soul, and by living continually in this realisation?

Hebrews 3;14 ''For we are made partakers of Christ (Truth) if we hold the beginning of our confidence steadfast unto the end. And **I will dwell** among the children of Israel and **will** not forsake my people Israel.''

1 Kings 6;13

And I will dwell among the children of
Israel, and will not forsake my people
Israel

Psalm 4:8
I will both lay me down in peace, and
sleep: for thou, Lord, only makes me
dwell in safety.

Psalm 23:6
Surely goodness and mercy shall follow
me all the days of my life: and I will
dwell in the house of the Lord forever.

Psalm 27:4
One thing have I desired of the Lord,
that will I seek after; that I may dwell in
the house of the Lord all the days of my
life, to behold the beauty of the Lord,
and to enquire in his temple.

Psalm 145:9
The Lord is good to all: and his tender mercies are over all his works.

Lamentations 3:22
It is of the Lord's mercies that we are not consumed because his compassions fail not.

Lamentations 3:32
But though he causes grief, yet will he have compassion according to the multitude of his mercies.

Matthew 4:23
And Jesus went about all Galilee, teaching in their synagogues, and preaching the gospel of the kingdom, and healing all manner of sickness and all manner of disease among the people.

Matthew 9:35
And Jesus went about all the cities and villages, teaching in their synagogues,

and preaching the gospel of the
kingdom, and healing every sickness
and every disease among the people.

Luke 9:6
And they departed, and went through
the towns, preaching the gospel, and
healing everywhere.

Luke 9:11
And the people, when they knew it,
followed him: and he received them,
and spoke unto them of the kingdom of
God, and healed them that had need of
healing.

Acts 4:22
For the man was above forty years old,
on whom this miracle of healing was
shewed.

Acts 10:38
How God anointed Jesus of Nazareth
with the Holy Ghost and with power:
who went about doing good and healing

all that were oppressed of the devil; for God was with him.

Jeremiah 29:11-13
For I know the thoughts that I think toward you, saith the Lord, thoughts of peace, and not of evil, to give you an expected end. Then shall ye call upon me, and ye shall go and pray unto me, and I will hearken unto you. And ye shall seek me and find me when ye shall search for me with all your heart.

Psalm 26:8
Lord, I have loved the habitation of thy house and the place where thine honour dwelleth.

Psalm 119:47
And I will delight myself in thy commandments, which I have loved.

Psalm 119:48
My hands also will I lift up unto thy commandments, which I have loved;

and I will meditate in thy statutes.

Isaiah 43:4
Since thou was precious in my sight,
thou hast been honourable and I have
loved thee: therefore will I give men for
thee, and people for thy life.

Jeremiah 2:25
Withhold thy foot from being unshod,
and thy throat from thirst: but thou said,
There is no hope: no; for I have loved
strangers, and after them will I go.

Jeremiah 14:10
Thus saith the Lord unto this people,
Thus have they loved to wander, they
have not refrained their feet, therefore
the Lord doth not accept them; he will
now remember their iniquity, and visit
their sins.

Jeremiah 31:3
The Lord hath appeared of old unto me,
saying, Yea, I have loved thee with an

everlasting love: therefore with loving
kindness have I drawn thee.

Malachi 1:2
I have loved you, saith the Lord. Yet ye
say Wherein hast thou loved us? Was
not Esau Jacob's brother? saith the
Lord: yet I loved Jacob,

Mark 10:21
Then Jesus beholding him loved him,
and said unto him, One thing thou
lackest: go thy way, sell whatsoever
thou hast, and give to the poor, and thou
shalt have treasure in heaven: and come,
take up the cross, and follow me.

John 3:16
For God so loved the world, that he
gave his only begotten Son, that
whosoever believeth in him should not
perish, but have everlasting life.

John 13:34
A new commandment I give unto you,

that ye love one another; as I have loved
you, that ye also love one another.

John 14:28
Ye have heard how I said unto you, I go
away, and come again unto you. If ye
loved me, ye would rejoice, because I
said, I go unto the Father: for my,
Father is greater than I.

John 15:9
As the Father hath loved me, so have I
loved you: continue ye in my love.

John 15:12
This is my commandment, That ye love
one another, as I have loved you.

John 16:27
For the Father himself loveth you,
because ye have loved me, and have
believed that I came out from God.

2 Chronicles 6:19
Have respect therefore to the prayer of
thy servant, and to his supplication, O

Lord my God, to hearken unto the cry
and the prayer which thy servant
prayeth before thee

Psalm 18:6
In my distress I called upon the Lord
and cried unto my God: he heard my
voice out of his temple, and my cry
came before him, even into his ears.

THE COINS OF CHRISTIAN SCIENCE

Gold
The silent thoughts of Truth and Love
which heal the sick
Silver
The spoken word of Truth and Love
which casts out evil and heals the sick
Currency
The written word of Truth and Love
published and distributed throughout the
world healing sickness and sin, but this
currency must be backed up by a gold
reserve in human   character

Prayers

You shall run and not be weary;
(to run- rise higher spiritually and not
react
not be weary, but rest in divine love and
not relapse)

Stay in your own home of demonstration.
Keep your peace for idle curiosity,
criticism, or even false sympathy may
lure you forth

From this hour I ordain myself loosed of
limits and imaginary lines
Going where I list, my own master total
and absolute,
Listening to others, considering well what
they say,
Pausing, searching, receiving,
contemplating,
Gently but with undeniable will divesting
myself of the holds that would hold me
Love flows through every avenue, fills
every channel and removes every
obstruction
No limits follow me for I am master of

my own

Prayer without ceasing is to live in the consciousness of one mind, one God.

Difference between belief and understanding:
Belief is a decision made from reasoning in material things, maybe the false conclusion
Understanding is a demonstrable knowledge obtained from a clear perception of the real and eternal

Trust in God- God is life

God is infinite, therefore if we are the image and likeness of infinity, we have no beginning and no end,

are his image and likeness,

that is my life insurance (Unknown)

Because I have put my trust in God, I have no responsibility whatsoever

My home is in God. I partake of the bounties of God's table spread with milk and honey of His kingdom.

I give no heed to what I shall say, to what I shall wear, or wherewith I shall pay my debt

Whatsoever I shall speak, God speaks through me

His word is of healing the nations, He clothes me with white garments of His own weaving- the robe of righteousness, eternal and indestructible

Truth is my income, is ever present and has wiped out my indebtedness

Truth and love flow freely without price

Oh!! God, I have taken hold of thy hand, of thine omnipotence

Thou hast taken my feet from the mire and clay and establish them upon a rock.

I am not afraid for I know thou hast lifted me above the world, its erroneous illusions, and temptations

I know them, henceforth no more forever

(Unknown)

Quotes from famous people

'' I learned that courage was not the absence of fear, but the triumph over it. The brave man is not he who does not feel afraid, but he who conquers that fear''. – Nelson Mandela

''Believe in yourself, take on your challenges, dig deep within yourself to conquer fears. Never let anyone bring you down. You have got to keep going. '' Chantal Sutherland

Life is 10% what happens to you and 90% how you react to it. Charles R. Swindoll

Optimism is the faith that leads to achievement. Nothing can be done without hope and confidence. Helen Keller

Change your life today. Don't gamble on the future, act now, without delay. Simone de Beauvoir

Infuse your life with action. Don't wait for it to happen. Make it happen. Make your own future. Make your own hope. Make your own love. And whatever your beliefs, honor your creator, not by passively waiting for grace to come down from upon high, but by doing what you can to make grace happen... yourself, right now, right down here on Earth.

 Bradley Whitford

We should not give up and we should not allow the problem to defeat us. A. P. J. Abdul Kalam

It does not matter how slowly you go as long as you do not stop. Confucius

Your talent is God's gift to you. What you do with it is your gift back to God. Leo Buscaglia

Our greatest weakness lies in giving up. The most certain way to succeed is always to try just one more time. Thomas A. Edison

Consult not your fears but your hopes and your dreams. Think not about your frustrations, but about your unfulfilled potential. Concern yourself not with what you tried and failed in, but with what it is still possible for you to do. Pope John XXIII

Perseverance is not a long race; it is
many short races one after the other.
Walter Elliot

When something is important
enough, you do it even if the odds are
not in your favor. Elon Musk

**Never give up for that is just the place
and time that the tide will turn**
Harriet Beecher Stowe

There is only one corner of the
universe you can be certain of
improving, and that's your own self.
Aldous Huxley

CHAPTER 11

Why my pain became my teacher

Before going through this challenge, I loved people but mostly I loved my immediate family members. I did not want anyone to say anything about them but with cancer, this all changed. I began to see people in a different way because of people dying around me every now and then, I thought that I could go anytime, die, without anyone stopping it. I was reminded to love the way Jesus taught us to love one another. Was it a sin or crime to love myself? Louise Hay spoke about it and this really started to make a difference in my thoughts and actions. I learnt to love and value myself. How do I look at other people if I do not know the inner Selina?

Through the study of other people's ways of healing, I came to understand that the only hurdle between perfect health and disease is hung on a simple system which I now use to help others. I call it ACTS system.

1. Accept/Acknowledge
2. Create
3. Take Action
4. Serve

Acceptance/acknowledgement

I learnt in this challenge that things happen for a reason and there is a purpose for it, to us and for us. When challenges come our way, we should learn to accept that things are the way they are for a reason and acknowledge that we are above problems. I found power in looking at them, accepting and acknowledging them but not giving them my power. This was brought home by the way things opened up. After I had been destroyed by chemotherapy, the Doctors looked for other ways to try and treat me. They wanted to get some bone marrow from any of my siblings who had the same blood group as me. In the UK I had only one brother, the rest are in the motherland, Africa.

My brother was no match. We sent for my other siblings to have their blood taken from the laboratory so that if they were found to be a match, they could come and help me out, that did not work either. It all went wrong to such an extent that some other people's names were written on the document, people I never knew. This worried the doctors and family members, but it never bothered me. I acknowledged that we had a challenge and accepted that there was no way at the moment, where humanly speaking, anything could be done. The inner me knew that they did not control my life and my purpose in this world. We all have purposes on this dimension, and it is only through learning from the great master, inner self, that we can reach and utilise our full potential. They did all they could until a time when they decided I should have Radiotherapy. This got me thinking and digging deeper and praying with other loving people, Faith and Brian from S.A, my CSP (Christian Science Practitioner) who never gave up on me. These were my torch bearers and their dedication and encouragement were second to none. I let go of fear and trusted God more. I stood at the door of my thoughts and chose what I could take on board into my being and throw away the rubbish. I knew I had the power to control myself in all this, so I just stood my ground and let things unfold. Power to the Creator, my God my all.

Create

Things started bombarding me as I came out of hospital from falling out with the system. I asked myself whether I was creating the right environment conducive to what I wanted to create in my life. I had to learn the art of giving and receiving. This is when I met a group of highly spiritual people who were working with Jean Houston. This group was my life saver, The Quantum Hearts. When I first got in touch, honestly, I was just waiting to die. I did not know how things were going to work out but was drawn to an online course Jean was offering. This was interaction, something to do to keep thoughts away from me.

We would skype every Sunday evening and did so for six months before I could lead the group prayers myself. When we started I did not have any hair, did not have any energy to sit up in a chair so used to do it from my bed. Within a short period of time I was strong and managed to be a partaker of what they were offering. I really know and understand the value of strong spiritual support system, people who believe that everything is possible.

Taking Action

I could have been given all the support I needed but if I had not taken action, I really could have flown away, died. I knew I had to do whatever it took for me to see results. I was introduced to some salad fast, smooth fast and prayer fasting. I held on to them so dearly because to be honest my life depended on it. I did not have any choice but to wait on it. MOA, a drink of 34 nutrients came into use. I liked the fact that the drink was full of organic nutrients that were all mixed together. I religiously started on it and continue to use it even now.

Prayer has always been my foundation so that is one thing I believe in. Without God I would be empty. He is my all and I am in awe of His love for me. I continue to search into my inner being to listen to his directions.

Serve

I found that by sharing what I found in my journey helps others and so have come up with the idea of giving to my community. I have a few people with whom I have shared what I did and as long as they listened they were helped or their relatives were released from the grip of fear.

Exercise

Steps to get what you want
This can be done in pairs or on your own:
Decide it - What do you want in your life?
Believe that it is possible
Feel it
See it

Romans 12:2 'And be not conformed to this world; but be transformed by the renewing of your mind, that ye may prove what is that good, and acceptable, and perfect, will of God'
To me it clearly means I have to detoxify my mind of the ills of this world and fill my mind with goodness. I am renewing my thoughts every

day, so I am sharing one of my affirmations with you.

Right here and right now, I am constructing a positive self-image
I see myself in the theatre of my mind, being, doing, and having all the good I desire
I AM HEALTHY
I AM HAPPY
I AM LOVING
I AM SUCCESFULL
I AM PROSPEROUS
I AM RICH
Thank you, Father,
Thank you God-in-me!!!
At the moment I am sharing my 3D System with the world, I have learnt to Detoxify, De-stress and Delete. We all need to work on our bodies, inner being, feed our thoughts, destressing and Deleting all the dead cells and thoughts which no longer serve us. I encourage everyone to work on themselves and feed their mind with new thoughts.

HAPPY JOURNEY TO SELF-HEALING, SELF-SERVING AND SERVING ALL

About The Author

Selina Mugodi Cheshire was born in a family of 9, 6 boys and 3 girls and is the middle child. From a young age she was taught by her father to care for the home and cook, clean and do most chores necessary to make a home functional. I was privileged in that it gave me a sense of independence and determination to better my life and not to depend on a man for up keep. At the age of 17, I went away from home and worked as a temporary teacher and I felt as if I was born to teach. I was given a class where ¾ of the children could hardly spend the whole week attending lessons but by the end of the year, 70% passed their exams. I developed a hunger for sharing and imparting knowledge to humanity.
While in hospital God told me to stop waiting for healing because I was already healed. He gave me a vision

where I was on a stage sharing His
goodness and so the Public Speaker
was born.